THIS IS ME! 2022

AWAY WITH WORDS

Edited By Andrew Porter

First published in Great Britain in 2022 by:

Young Writers
Remus House
Coltsfoot Drive
Peterborough
PE2 9BF
Telephone: 01733 890066
Website: www.youngwriters.co.uk

All Rights Reserved
Book Design by Ashley Janson
© Copyright Contributors 2022
Softback ISBN 978-1-80459-004-1

Printed and bound in the UK by BookPrintingUK
Website: www.bookprintinguk.com
YB0506YZ

FOREWORD

For Young Writers' latest competition This Is Me, we asked primary school pupils to look inside themselves, to think about what makes them unique, and then write a poem about it! They rose to the challenge magnificently and the result is this fantastic collection of poems in a variety of poetic styles.

Here at Young Writers our aim is to encourage creativity in children and to inspire a love of the written word, so it's great to get such an amazing response, with some absolutely fantastic poems. It's important for children to focus on and celebrate themselves and this competition allowed them to write freely and honestly, celebrating what makes them great, expressing their hopes and fears, or simply writing about their favourite things. This Is Me gave them the power of words. The result is a collection of inspirational and moving poems that also showcase their creativity and writing ability.

I'd like to congratulate all the young poets in this anthology, I hope this inspires them to continue with their creative writing.

CONTENTS

Heronsgate School, Walnut Tree

Phoebe Graham (11)	1
Faridat Shouaib (11)	2
Eve Palkauskaite (8)	4
Zane Salako (10)	6
Finley Toomer (10)	8
Poppy Todman (10)	10
Ali Zain Master (10)	12
Anushka Prasher (10)	14
Isla Thomson (8)	15
Emily Skells (11)	16
Thomas McEwan (11)	17
Neeyu Sung (11)	18
Zubaida Begum (10)	20
Kai Nicholls (11)	22
Mia Houghton (9)	23
Sophie Ball (11)	24
Charlie Fenton (10)	26
Marvin Bagnall (11)	27
Eric Machiquez Reay (11)	28
Ava Omonayajo (11)	29
James Underwood (11)	30
Lizzie Nowik (11)	31
Abbaasali Hussein (10)	32
Elgin Agyemang (11)	33
Brooke Dawson (11)	34
Benjamin Forsyth (10)	35
Alfie Cvjetkovic (10)	36
Amy Green (11)	37
David Yadua (11)	38
Reece Tambe (10)	39
Everly Wright (9)	40
Izzy Headland (10)	41
Szymon Szutkowski (11)	42
Niamh Hawkins (11)	43
Naomi Chimwayange (8)	44
Benjamin Strydom (10)	45
Janice Yuen (11)	46
Akpene Atsutse (11)	47
Nicholas Galvin (11)	48
Amelia Scott (11)	49
Fredrick Cheong (11)	50
Omar Ahmed (11)	51
Izzy Healy (9)	52
Micah Akande (10)	53
Riley Carson (10)	54
Louisa Hammond (8)	55
Archie Beaver (10)	56
Thale Clark (8)	57
Muhammed-Haadi Somji (11)	58
Alicja Jaszczyk (10)	59
Stacy Kanu (11)	60
Kimani Njogu (8)	61
Theadora Hyne (7)	62
Woody Ford (8)	63
Morgan Roberts-Fennemore (11)	64
Zachary Smith (11)	65
Rubi Green (10)	66
Zakary Peach (11)	67
Kristo Kocka (10)	68
Alexis-Mai Smith (11)	69
Ethan Duncan-Batt (10)	70
Holly Gregory (11)	71
Ruby Mccloud (9)	72
Adam Witkowski (10)	73
Luca Eggleston (10)	74
Mayson Moore-Kennett (8)	75
Melissa Morris (10)	76
Cianne-Lea Mahoney (8)	77
Adrian Szymkowiak (9)	78

Name	Number
Klaudia Gajewska (11)	79
Evie Wakeman (9)	80
Mason Willimott (8)	81
Beau Craig (10)	82
Murad Elfadaly (9)	83
Lauren Maynard (9)	84
Leo King (10)	85
Alex Bosco (10)	86
Ella Mowbray (8)	87
Neferah Jaunbocus (10)	88
Armaan Malik (8)	89
Adrianna Tryzna (7)	90
Max S C Coburn (11)	91
Isaac Jones (10)	92
Holly Dungar-Bullock (8)	93
Grace (7)	94
Tyler Howell (10)	95
Jasmine Saidi (11)	96
Amelia Omonayajo (7)	97
Theresa Wilson (7)	98
Lewis Chaproniere McLean (11)	99
Lilly Bernatowicz (7)	100
Sofia Brown (9)	101
Leyah Fisher (9)	102
Theo Smith (8)	103
Millie Beaver (9)	104
Isaac True (11)	105
Thomas Broad (9)	106
Firdaus Shouaib (8)	107
Thalia-Mae Simpson (11)	108
Aaron Gunasekara (8)	109
Bella Harris (7)	110
Jada Boyd (11)	111
Thiea Smith (8)	112
Petros Gkerdouki (11)	113
Ebony Davy (8)	114
Florence Stratford (8)	115
Alec Price (11)	116
Charlotte Goodwin (9)	117
Ben Evans (8)	118
Lennon Flynn (8)	119
William Galvin (7)	120
Jack Goldsmith (8)	121
Leila-Rae Llewellyn (7)	122
Arjun Prasher (8)	123
Harrison White (8)	124
Nia Shoko (8)	125
Jonathan Cane (9)	126
Vinnie Girdlestone (11)	127
James Diblasio (11)	128
Evie Hutchison (8)	129
Henry Ives (9)	130
Anna Knight (8)	131
Steffy Njenga (9)	132
Takuma Kozaki (8)	133
Ollie Reynolds (9)	134
Fatimah Mohammedali (8)	135
Sophia Sepehrtaj	136
Tommy Crouch (8)	137
Spyros Gkouma (9)	138
Zenon Murray (7)	139
Emma Shepherd (9)	140
Aoife Ramharack (9)	141
Noah Pykett (11)	142
Arvin Sandha (9)	143
Connor Perry (11)	144
Mia Beamont (9)	145
Mirella Biro Zengay (9)	146
Jenson Berry (8)	147
Stefania Dzopko (8)	148
Tyler Mossman (9)	149
Ruby Creaser (8)	150
Harun Abdalla (11)	151
Jacob-Junior Szukalski (7)	152
Tristan Marshall (9)	153
Dhruvan Ravi (8)	154
Adam Martisius (8)	155
Fortnum Brierley (8)	156
Alayna Afzal (7)	157
Nadia Ceglarz (9)	158
Jessica Foldesi (8)	159
Eve Selley (8)	160
Markus Kuhle (8)	161
Xander Smith (7)	162
Oscar Masterson (9)	163
George Orr (7)	164

Ollie Harrison (8)	165
Chi Yuet Sharon Shum (7)	166
May Chen (7)	167
Fadil Said (9)	168

Khalsa (VA) Primary School, Southall

Unika Davina Parmar (10)	169
Gunraj Talwar (9)	170
Taranjot Kaur Thind (10)	172
Harleen Chawala (9)	174
Gurjot Singh Chana (10)	175
Jaskeeratpal Kaur (10)	176
Sargun Khaneja (8)	177
Jaskirat Dhaliwal (10)	178
Harveen Kaur Marwa (9)	179
Amarleen Kaur Chopra (11)	180
Snehdeep Kaur Dhaliwal (10)	181
Anika Sethi (11)	182
Anishka Kaur Madan (9)	183
Harleen Kaur (9)	184
Mineet Kaur Chopra (10)	185
Ashmin Kaur Kukreja (9) & Baninder	186
Simran Dhillon (10)	187
Japleen Kaur Kubar (8)	188
Esher Bhogal	189
Divleen Kaur Khurana (9)	190
Mahek Khosla (9)	191
Mehar Moore (8)	192

Parkhall Primary School, Antrim

Alex Sanders (9)	193
Chester Moore (9)	194
Mollie Craig (9)	195
Caitlin Taylor (10)	196
Lewis Nicholl (10)	197
Louella McAleese (10)	198
Logan Wright (10)	199
Chloe Hurley (10)	200
Felicity Tarr (10)	201
Lexie Sloan (9)	202
Amiee McDonnell (10)	203

THE POEMS

I Am Phoebe Graham

I am my mum Karen and my dad Mathew who always help me.
I am my annoying but kind siblings Hermione, Leilani and Malaki.
I am my dogs Chewie, Lenny and Monty who always make me smile.
I am my grandparents who always make me excited to see them.
I am my friends who are always there.
I am my best friend Emily who always makes me bounce off the walls and go crazy.
I am the little things that make me happy like frogs and avocados.
I am the virus Covid-19 who made us all stay home from school and work for about two years.
I am the person who has never been in hospital for any injury even though I always have one.
I am my aunt who had a tumour in her mouth and now can barely talk without dentures.
I am my nan who is in and out of hospital all the time and is on medication.
I am Phoebe Serenity Graham and I am who I am, I am funny, kind, caring, artistic, creative, imaginative, unique and good with others.

Phoebe Graham (11)
Heronsgate School, Walnut Tree

I Am Me!

I am caring.
I am honest.
I'm not selfish.
I'm not rude.
I am clumsy.
I'm not unkind.

I know how the devastating World Wars started.
I don't know why glitter is shiny.
I know why February has fewer days than other months.
I don't know why parrots are colourful.
I know how to write amazing stories.
I don't know where flowers get their names from.

I am my clever dad who taught me how to deal with things.
I am my thoughtful mum who showed me how to be kind.
I am my marvellous sister who helped me whenever I need it.
I am my special friends who taught me to be hilarious.

I am my teachers who taught me how to write outstanding stories.

I once fell out of a plane!
I am the best artist ever!
I once was swallowed by a vicious shark!
I am the best story writer!

I am Faridat...
My name means unique.
I am who I am because of everyone
And that's what makes me... me!

Faridat Shouaib (11)
Heronsgate School, Walnut Tree

Friends And Family

F riends keep me company and make me happy.
R ight or wrong they always correct me.
I am really lonely when they aren't there.
E very time I'm feeling sad they always cheer me up.
N o one is better in my life except my family.
D o not cry when they are there.
S o when they are there I will always be happy.

A nd when they aren't there I will make new friends.
N ow I will always be happy even when they aren't there.
D rawing, their drawings are so wonderful.

F amily, oh my family, they are the ones I love most.
A teaspoon of trust is always in my family.
M y mum and dad respect me the most.
I love them so much, I wish they were always there.
L ove more and more when they do something nice.
Y ou and me and the people who read this poem, I hope I become friends with you next!

Eve Palkauskaite (8)
Heronsgate School, Walnut Tree

I Am Unique

I am my mum and dad who always supported me and still do.
I am my sister who always made me laugh and strive for greatness.
I am the doctor that helped me when I broke my arm.
I am bracelets that I lost at school.
I am the three friends that made me be great.
I am my teachers that inspired me every day.
I am my music teacher who gave me a spot in a concert.
I am the friends that I have left behind.
I am funny, I am thoughtful, I am smart, I am generous, I am diligent, I am ambitious and I am adventurous
But I have faults, I get mad, I can be annoying and I'm afraid of the dark
But with all of my faults I am unique.
I am Zane Salako and I am who I am because of everyone
Because of my faults and because I never give up
Because nothing will stop me when I set my mind to it

Not Covid, not sickle cells and definitely not myself
I am unique, I am who I am because of everyone.

Zane Salako (10)
Heronsgate School, Walnut Tree

Me, Myself And I

I am competitive.
I am not horrible.
I am sporty.
I am not selfish.

I am good at parkour.
I am amazing at Fortnite.
I am brilliant at football.
I am superb at gaming.

I know if you travel at the speed of light it takes you eight minutes to get to the sun.
I know why chameleons change colours.
I know how WWI and WWII started.
I know why leaves are the colour they are.

I got brought back from the dead.
I can't die.
I got tormented by a rhino.
I can fly.
My dog is made of glue.

I am the best at football.
I am the best at Fortnite.
I am the best at parkour.

I don't know why we can't think of a new colour.
I don't know why galaxies are colourful.
I am Finley...
My name means fair warrior and hero.
That is what makes me... me!

Finley Toomer (10)
Heronsgate School, Walnut Tree

I Am... Me

I have beautiful brown hair.
I don't have lots of money.
I have beautiful brown eyes.
I don't bully.
I have beautiful friends.
I don't tell people, "You're not good enough."

I am brave.
I am not rich.
I am talented.
I am not rude.
I am smart.
I am not someone to avoid.

I know yeast is alive.
I don't know why hyenas laugh.
I know you use 200 muscles to take a step.
I don't know why parrots are colourful.
I know you have over 600 muscles in your body.
I don't know why dolphins leap.

I am clumsy.
I am not always considerate.
I am emotional.
I am not always content.
I am different.
I am not perfect.

I am Poppy.
I am a stream of happiness.
My name means milk of happiness.
That makes me who I am.

Poppy Todman (10)
Heronsgate School, Walnut Tree

This Is Who I Am

I'm kind,
I'm not a liar,
I'm generous,
I'm not disrespectful,
I'm polite,
I'm not rude,
I'm honest,
I'm not weak.

I've travelled the world,
I'm as smart as can be,
I'm a great sportsman,
I'm as lucky as can be.

I may never see my dreams come true,
But I'll try my best to see them grow like vines,
I may not stay with my friends today,
But they will always be in my heart till I die.

I know why sugar is sweet,
I know why leaves are green,
I know why the sea is blue,
I know why clouds are grey.

I know my name is Ali,
My name means high-elevated champion,
I am a leader,
I am a debater,
I am who I am because of you.

Ali Zain Master (10)
Heronsgate School, Walnut Tree

I Am...

I am my dad, Aman, for teaching me how to bike.
I am my mom, Shruti, for getting me ready for school and swimming.
I am my dadi mama for giving me a cooking set and love.
I am my dadu for teaching me how to play chess.
I am my brother, Arjun for teaching me what love and laughter is.
I am my swimming coach Angela, for pushing me on.
I am my friends Ajla and Emaan for teaching me what friendship is.
I am my cousins Aryan and Krishiv for getting me into gaming.
I am my other cousin Nandu for getting me into art.
I am my sensei Pete for making me try my best.
I am my best friend Janice for solving maths problems with me.
I am Anushka Prasher, and this year I passed my 11+.
I am who I am because of everyone around me.

Anushka Prasher (10)
Heronsgate School, Walnut Tree

My Pets That I Adore

These are my pets I adore.
They are my fluffy friends.
I love them so much, they are the best.
Let's start with Hazel my hamster.
Cute and soft, Hazel has her own five-storey cage.
My dad likes to hold her and play with her.
Now my cat Poppy, she's my favourite, super soft.
Adorable with black and white splotches of fur.
A loud meow Poppy has, she makes it cute.
Poppy is super tiny and thin, she doesn't eat much.
Olaf, my other cat, is my sister's favourite pet.
He's super chunky, we want Olaf to eat less and
Poppy to eat more!
Olaf is literally Olaf from Frozen, he has three black
spots.
Now the weird part, we call Olaf guddy woo,
Or just oooo, my sister came up with peculiar
names!

Isla Thomson (8)
Heronsgate School, Walnut Tree

Who Am I?

I am my father who built me my bike when I was only two!
And my mother who took care of me when I was sick.
I am my two annoying siblings that never leave me alone.
I am my great grandfather who fought in the war but didn't make it.
Also my great grandmother who was a nurse and treated his wounds.
I am the girl who broke her ankle in Year 3 and didn't tell a teacher, oops!
I am all my friends who helped me when I needed them the most.
I am my amazing pre-school teacher who drove me home when my parents couldn't pick me up!
And Mr Dobson who is helping me through Year 6.
I am the girl who has had Covid-19 twice.
I am Emily Skells and I plan to live a long, happy life!
I am who I am because of everyone!

Emily Skells (11)
Heronsgate School, Walnut Tree

My Life

I am my mum Rachel who looked after me.
And my father Ian who made me laugh.
I am my nurses who helped me survive my early life and enabled me to walk when I was born.
And my grandma who visited me in hospital even though she was dying herself.
I am the doctor who said I wouldn't make it because of my disability.

I am my sister who loved me as soon as she was born.
And I am my physiotherapist who strengthened my legs.
I am my grandad Will who left Northern Ireland to start a better life with my grandma.
I am my dog Jake who reminded me to love the outside again and the joy in life.
I am my other grandad Malcom who died during Covid happily in his home.
I am who I am because of everyone.

Thomas McEwan (11)
Heronsgate School, Walnut Tree

My Life

I am silly,
I am caring,
I am clumsy,
I am calm... most of the time.

I'm not courageous,
I have no patience,
I can't tolerate bad smells,
I'm not good at English.

I know a bit of octopus biology,
I know how to build Minecraft structures,
I can assume that life can thrive on other planets,
I can assume what they look like.

I'm the man that taught himself art,
I'm the man that taught himself how to build,
I'm the man that hated homework,
I'm the man that didn't enjoy English.

I am Neeyu,
And I may be small but I'm just as equal as any of you,
But just remember,
Some great things can come in small packages.

Neeyu Sung (11)
Heronsgate School, Walnut Tree

Zubaida, Like Cream!

I am beserk
But I am not delusional.
I am thoughtful
But I am not selfish.
I am passionate
But I am not horrible.
I am Zubaida.

I know why no tears come out when babies cry.
I know how colours form on butterflies.
I know when people start to lie.

I am snack gucy.
I am divine.
I am creative.
I am lovely.
I am beautiful.
I am brave.
I am me.

I am my Year Six teacher who told me to keep going.
I am my friends who keep my emotions flowing.
I am my mum who showed me what love is.
I am my dad who told me to try exotic things.

I am Zubaida.
I am soft-bodied, like cream
And I am who I am because of everyone around me!

Zubaida Begum (10)
Heronsgate School, Walnut Tree

Kai And Only Kai

I am sporty
I am not great at maths
I am good at football
I am not confident talking out loud to the class
I am clumsy
I am not selfish
I am intelligent.

I know why World War I and II started
I know what my name means
I know where cocoa comes from
I know where the German soldiers are buried.

I am my auntie who looked after me
I am my mum who gave birth to me
I am my dad who taught me how to play football
I am James D and Harun who are there for me when I'm down
I am my teacher who helps me learn.

I am Kai
And I'm a 'seashell warrior'
I am a guardian and that's what makes me, me.

Kai Nicholls (11)
Heronsgate School, Walnut Tree

This Is Me

Me, you want to know about me?
Well, I love animals
Like the waggy tail and feet mixed together
And that big fluffball with green eyes
They make me smile when I can't hold myself up and I don't feel my best.

I can get sad but my dad makes me smile
But if he can't, my grandpa always does
And he is better than my dad sometimes
But my dad can do it himself most of the time.

Annoying my brother, I do it sometimes
But we're friends and both of us play with our plastic bricks called Lego
But my fluffball normally breaks our buildings
Like the Black Panther, she is
This is me.

Mia Houghton (9)
Heronsgate School, Walnut Tree

I Am Sophie!

I am hungry
I am proud
I am divine
I am creative.

I haven't got blonde hair
I haven't got a perfect life
I haven't got the best art
I haven't got the best writing.

I am the roly-poly that broke my wrist
I am my mum who looks after me
I am my teacher who is always there for me
I am my friends who are always there for me.

I like Roblox which is always fun!
I love my resilient grandparents
I like my class who are full of personality
I love my sister, Emily, who always makes me happy.

I am wise and creative
I am the world around me
And that's what makes me... me!

Sophie Ball (11)
Heronsgate School, Walnut Tree

I Am Who I Am

I am my mum Michelle, who brought me into this world and cared for me.
I am my dad Ian, who is always supportive and puts me on the right lines.
I am my older brothers, Brandon and Cameron who are amazing.
I am my dog Milo, who always cheers me up when I am sad.
I am my amazing teachers, Miss King, Mr Dobson, Mr Jones and Mr Wilson who helped my education.
I am my very first trip to Spain, which made me love flying!
I am my amazing football coach Ian, (my dad) who helped me get better at football.
I am the NHS, who help thousands during Covid-19.
I am Charlie Fenton.
I am who I am because of everyone.

Charlie Fenton (10)
Heronsgate School, Walnut Tree

Marvin Is Hungry

I am hungry.
I am kind.
I am not competitive.
I am sometimes funny.
I am sometimes not funny.
I am me.
I am a better basketball player than Lebron James.
I am an athlete.
I am the funniest comedian in the world.
My dad is a bodybuilder.
I am a professional artist.
I am my mum who brought me up.
I am my dad who taught me the things of the world.
I am my annoying sisters who never leave me alone.
I am my loud brother who doesn't know how to stop yapping.
I am my friends who are always there for me.
I am Marvin Bagnall. My name means lover of the sea.
I am me.

Marvin Bagnall (11)
Heronsgate School, Walnut Tree

This Is Me

I am clumsy
I am not selfish
I am nosy
I am not a liker of school
I am a PC gamer
I am not a cheese lover.

I speak fluent Spanish
I know my name stands for 'forever ruler'
I don't know trigonometry
I don't know how Gummy Bears are produced.

I am the best at Fortnite
I am a professional gamer
I am the smartest.

I am my friends, who pushed me to reach my goals
I am my teacher, who tells me not to rush
I am my mother, who gave birth to me
I am my dad, who helps me and entertains me.

I am a forever ruler, and this is me.

Eric Machiquez Reay (11)
Heronsgate School, Walnut Tree

I Am...

I am my mum, who made me smile every day,
I am my sisters, Aisha, Amelia and Aliza,
I am my dad, who understood my troubles,
I am my teacher, who taught me to be independent,
I am my friends, for caring,
I am my cousin, for teaching me to take challenges,
I am my grandma, for saying it's okay to be different,
I am the bullies, who stopped my journey,
I am the people, who looked at me funny,
I am my grandpa, who is up in the sky.

I am Ava Omonayajo
And I found out that people could bully you because of your differences,
I am who I am because of everyone.

Ava Omonayajo (11)
Heronsgate School, Walnut Tree

I Am...

I am my mum who gave me my eyes
I am my dad who gave me my smile
I am my friends Zach and David who make me laugh
And my auntie and uncle who gave me my sketchbook
I am Miss Potter who helped me through rough times
I am the doctor who helped me when I nearly died
I am my grampy who encouraged me when I did my magic tricks
And my nana who gave me my cooking ability
I am Chandler from Friends who gave me my humour
I am my cousin who gave me my coolness
And my coaches who assisted me in football
I am James Underwood
I am who I am because of everyone.

James Underwood (11)
Heronsgate School, Walnut Tree

The Eponymous Oath

I am competitive
I'm not secluded
I am optimistic
I'm not negative
I am visionary
I'm not boring.

I know how the war started
I don't know why parrots mimic
I know why leaves are green
I don't know why giraffes have long necks.

I am my nan who brought me into baking
I am my dad who brought me into sports
I am my mum who made me who I am.

I've been bitten by a shark
I've swam through the ocean
I've jumped out of a plane.

I am Lizzie the oath, the promise and this is me.

Lizzie Nowik (11)
Heronsgate School, Walnut Tree

I Am Abbaasali Hussein

I am my incredible mother, Roshina, who is the kindest person I know.
I am my siblings, who are very caring.
I am my football coach, George, who has taught me the skills and tricks
And my encouraging father, who always pushes me to my limit.
I am my grandma, who prays for me, so I am safe.
I am my friends, Zak and Nickl, who always stand up for me.
I am my neighbours, who play with me in the car park.
I am the incredible Abbaasali Hussein
And last year, I sent my team to the knockouts with a bullet header at the back post.
I am who I am, because of everyone!

Abbaasali Hussein (10)
Heronsgate School, Walnut Tree

Who Am I?

I am my mother, Emma, who travelled to England,
I am my father, Eric, who served twenty-two years in the army then moved to England,
I am my brother, Tyrone, who made my life interesting,
I am my mother, Emma, who travelled back to Ghana,
I am my cousins, aunties and my fairy godmother and my uncle, who gave me the African experiences,
I am my brother, Tyrone, who got me into science and history,
I am my doctor, who treated my malaria,
I am my best friends, who I left behind to travel to England,
My name is Elgin Agyemang and I am who I am because of everyone.

Elgin Agyemang (11)
Heronsgate School, Walnut Tree

This Is Me

I am my lovely mother, Gill.
I am my beautiful sisters, Tegan and Charlotte.
I am my strong nanny, Pat, who always told me to be careful.
I am my determined dad who got me into kickboxing.
I am my helpful auntie who was there for my mum.
I am my talented nanny, Barbara, who helped me with my drawing.
I am my caring nan-nan who looked after me lots.
I am my inspirational teacher who helped me with my learning.
I am my encouraging kickboxing instructor who taught me kickboxing.
I am the amazing Brooke Dawson
And I am who I am because of everyone.

Brooke Dawson (11)
Heronsgate School, Walnut Tree

I Am Benji Forsyth

I am my mother Kirsty and my father Stuart.
I am my brother Jacob, who picked me up when I was down.
I am my grandparents, whose house I celebrated my first ever birthday at.
I am my cat Belle, who taught me what it's like to have a pet.
I am the jellyfish that stung my leg in Thailand and the doctor who patched it up.
I am the boy who stayed locked up in my home for a fifth of my life.
I am my friend who I've known for eight years.
I am the football player who broke my wrist and then helped me up again.
I am who I am because of everyone!

Benjamin Forsyth (10)
Heronsgate School, Walnut Tree

I Am...

I am my dad, Alex, who got me into sports and made me laugh every day.
I am my mum, Zara, who looked after me and asked me if I was okay every day.
I am my sisters, Ella, Kacie and my brother, Callum, who played games with me every day.
I am the boy who came last in his basketball tournament but it encouraged me to get better.
I am my nan, Irene, who died when I was eight.
I am the doctor who cleaned my huge cut and stopped the bleeding.
I am Alfie and I'm the boy who has been through Covid and many more things.
I am who I am because of everyone.

Alfie Cvjetkovic (10)
Heronsgate School, Walnut Tree

This Is Me

I am my mum who always cared for me,
I am my dad who always made me smile,
I am my brother who always protected me,
I am my cousin who always played with me,
I am my hamster, Oreo, AKA Floof, who always made me happy,
I am my friends who made me laugh,
I am my teachers who always supported and believed in me,
I am the authors who wrote the books that inspire me,
I am Covid who stayed for almost three years but humbled me and made me more grateful,
I am the holidays I always looked forward to.

I am who I am because of everyone.

Amy Green (11)
Heronsgate School, Walnut Tree

I Am...

I am my mum, who raised the money for me to come to this country.

I am my aunty, who encouraged me to practise the piano.

I am Mrs Richards, for teaching me how to play 'Happy Birthday' for my dad's birthday.

I am my dad, who teaches me football skills at the weekends.

I am my sister, who constantly makes me laugh and smile.

I am my teacher, Mrs Timmins, who teaches me several methods of percentages.

I am David Oreoluwa Yadua, and last year I was awarded a gold medal for my composition in piano.

I am who I am because of everyone!

David Yadua (11)
Heronsgate School, Walnut Tree

This Is Me!

I am my caring mother, Ade, who gave birth to me.
I am my amazing dad, Kingsley, who takes me to football training.
I am my wonderful brother, Ethan, who plays football with me.
I am my nice sister, who helped me when I needed it.
I am my happy friend, who helps me with my training,
I am my honest neighbour, who comes over when needed.
I am my football team and coach, who supports me and teaches me some tricks.
I am my great doctor, who takes care of me when I am hurt.
I am Reece Tambe, and I am who I am because of everyone!

Reece Tambe (10)
Heronsgate School, Walnut Tree

Everly

E xciting memories hanging with friends.
V ery difficult sometimes but also easy.
E njoying new things at school with friends.
R elying on friends to grow.
L oves laughs with friends.
Y ou're only this age for once.

W onderful times made with friends.
R espect one another.
I ncredible dreams come true if you listen.
G reat listening makes teamwork.
H elpful teachers help children learn.
T his is my story about school life.

Everly Wright (9)
Heronsgate School, Walnut Tree

I Am...

I am my mum, for teaching me netball.
I am Krystian, my mum's partner, for listening to me play the keyboard.
I am my teacher and my class, for welcoming me.
I am my friend, Jasmine, for teaching me shooting in netball.
I am my nan, for talking to me.
I am my grandad, for teaching me jokes.
I am my friend, Nefirah, for blocking during netball.
I am my netball team, for supporting me.
I am my friends, for helping me.
I am Izzy Headland and I can be anything I want to be.
I am who I am because of everyone.

Izzy Headland (10)
Heronsgate School, Walnut Tree

I Am Szymon

I am my mom, Kamila, who raised me to be here since I was young.
I am my dad, Radoslaw, who inspired me from young to now.
I am my brother, Dawid, who encouraged me to do everything I ever wanted to do and to try my best.
I am Covid-19 which took over my life and skipped months of learning.
I am my friend who helps me do stuff in football.
I am my football coach who made me as good as I am today.
I am the people who encouraged my family to move to England for better education.
I am who I am today because of everyone.

Szymon Szutkowski (11)
Heronsgate School, Walnut Tree

I Am Who I Am

I am my mother, who taught me perseverance.
I am my father, who encouraged me to do my homework.
I am my sister, who taught me to control my feelings.
I am my half-brother, who showed me that gaming with other people is fun.
I am my nan, who taught me generosity.
I am my grandfather, who has a love for technology.
I am my auntie, who taught me kindness.
I am my friends, who make me happy.

I am Niamh Hawkins, bright and radiant.
I am who I am because of the people I have encountered and known.

Niamh Hawkins (11)
Heronsgate School, Walnut Tree

Naomi Chimwayange

N aughty but only at home
A rtistic everywhere
O pera singer all the time
M ajestic and magical
I ntelligent, also smart.

C ute and calm
H yper but honest
I ndestructible and encouraging
M arvellous and magnificent
W riter, I love the weekend
A mazing, I like angels
Y oung but nine years old
A crobatic and love bananas
N ice and naughty
G irl and graceful
E nergetic.

Naomi Chimwayange (8)
Heronsgate School, Walnut Tree

This Is Me

I am my mum, Tarryn, who has helped me through everything.
I am my dad, Dylan, who spent as much time with me as he could.
I am the doctor who kept me alive when I had pneumonia as a baby.
I am my best friend, Keagan, who helped me do things,
I am the friend who was there when my dad died.
I am the man who taught me how to ski and then the next day I broke my wrist.
I am my teachers, especially Mr Dobson who has told me a lot of secrets about the RAF and is really funny.
I am who I am because of everyone.

Benjamin Strydom (10)
Heronsgate School, Walnut Tree

I Am...

I am my mum, who cares about me most,
I am my brother, who brings laughter to me,
I am my granny, who comforted me when I was sad,
I am my grandpa, who taught me how to use chopsticks,
I am my teacher, who helped me to learn piano,
I am the lady, who brought me into the art world,
I am my teacher, Mrs Timmins, who gives me support,
I am my best friend, Anushka, who solves maths problems with me,
I am my friend, Kayley, who helped me go through my hard times,
I am who I am, because of everyone.

Janice Yuen (11)
Heronsgate School, Walnut Tree

This Is Me!

I am my mother, Grace, who keeps on inspiring me every day.
I am my dad, Benjamin, who keeps on teaching me new things every day.
I am my grandad, who was my only grandad but died during Covid.
I am the girl who gets hate comments sometimes.
I am Covid which taught me that money doesn't grow on trees, you have to earn it.
I am the girl who fell off a hill trying to ride a bike.
I am my best friends Lexi, Phoebe, Stacy and Alfie, who changed my life forever.
I am who I am because of everyone.

Akpene Atsutse (11)
Heronsgate School, Walnut Tree

I Am Myself

I am my lovely mother Dani, who helped me through lots.
I am my dad Tony, who introduced me to football.
I am my brother Will, who entertains me.
I am my friend Zak, a really funny guy.
I am my football team, the calm and composed.
I am my neighbours, always there with a spare key.
I am my pets, knowing when I'm down.
I am my grandparents, who taught me generosity.
I am Nicholas Galvin
And last year I helped my football team up a division.
I am who I am because of everyone.

Nicholas Galvin (11)
Heronsgate School, Walnut Tree

I Am Amelia Scott

I am my mum, Michelle, who is always loving.
I am my dad, Kevin, who is a great dad.
I am the coach who didn't catch me when I fell off the beam.
I am the doctors who put my leg in a cast.
I am my friends who always make me laugh.
I am my coach, Beth, who gained my confidence back.
I am my cousins who always make me happy.
I am my school who taught me everything I need to know.
I am my grandad, Brian, who always makes me feel special.
I am who I am because of everyone.

Amelia Scott (11)
Heronsgate School, Walnut Tree

Who Am I?

I am my mum who cooks food for me every day.
I am my cousins who go to the park with me always,
And my uncle who taught me to cycle.
I am the doctor who helped me when I broke my right hand.
I am my brother Garrick who plays with me every day.
I am my coach who taught me to do tae kwon do,
And the judge who gave me my red belt.
I am my parents who decided to move here from Hong Kong.
I am the pilot of the flight which brought me here.
I am who I am because of everyone.

Fredrick Cheong (11)
Heronsgate School, Walnut Tree

I Am - I Am Not

My name is Omar and my name means flourishing and long living
I am funny
I am not perfect
I am passionate
I am not always happy
I am a friendly human
I am not the best, I try and make the right choices
I know that my name means flourishing and long living
I don't know why giraffes are so tall
I do know why leaves are green
I don't know why pens use lots of ink
I am the best bike rider
I like being funny
I am Omar, this is what makes me, me.

Omar Ahmed (11)
Heronsgate School, Walnut Tree

Happiness

When I come home from school
I want to go in a pool
But it feels like a pool of drool
When I see my dog she greets me in the best way
That just makes me sway.
But that isn't all
My family is always there for me to get to football
I am a box of tricks
Just like a little pip.
I love food just like my family
I don't really care as long as my family's there
Also I love Lego so much
My room is a Lego shop
My sister's is a cuddle shop.

Izzy Healy (9)
Heronsgate School, Walnut Tree

I Am Micah

I am my father, and my mother, who have always supported my creativity and pushed me.
I am my dog and cat who keep me jovial.
I am the doctor who cured me of pneumonia when I was three.
I am the piano teacher who inspired me to play the piano.
I am the nurse who stitched my head wound when I was eight.
I am my brother who helped me learn how to code.
I am my teacher who helped to get 100% on my mock SATs.
I am Micah Akande and I am who I am because of everyone!

Micah Akande (10)
Heronsgate School, Walnut Tree

I Am Riley

I am good at drawing.
I am bad at maths.
I am an animal lover.
I know what cheese is made of.
I know why my eyes are light brown.
I know why the sky's blue.
I don't know why some people litter.
I don't know how red cheese is made.
I enjoy being happy.
I enjoy being in my room.
I enjoy reading.
I enjoy seeing a teacher Mrs Smith.
I enjoy seeing my dad and mum.
I enjoy swimming.
And that's what makes me... me!

Riley Carson (10)
Heronsgate School, Walnut Tree

I Am Accident Prone

Once when I was in foundation I cracked my head open.
Once in foundation I slipped in a puddle.
Once in foundation I lost all my plasters.
Once in Year 1 I broke my arm.
Once in Year 1 I fell off the Eiffel Tower.
Once in Year 1 I banged my leg on the wall.
Once in Year 2 I twisted my ankle.
Once in Year 2 I nearly broke my finger.
Now I am in Year 3, I said I want to break my leg.
Now I am in Year 3, I scraped my knee again.
This is me.

Louisa Hammond (8)
Heronsgate School, Walnut Tree

I Am Archie Beaver

I am my caring mum, who created me.
I am my honest dad, who taught me how to answer a hard question.
I am my kind uncle, who always invites me to Christmas dinner
And my hard-working grandad, who taught me all about cars.
I am my forgiving nan, who always helped me with my hard homework.
I am my creative aunt, who is always there for me
And my smart teacher, who gets me to understand things.
I am Archie Beaver.
I am who I am because of everyone!

Archie Beaver (10)
Heronsgate School, Walnut Tree

About Me!

This is about me:
I don't like cats because they play with rats.
I also hate dirt 'cause it messes up your skirt.
However I love dogs 'cause they're so cute when they sit on logs.
And I also love bats 'cause they scare away the rats.
But I hate the dark but love when dogs bark.
I also hate rain and when your money falls down the drain.

So this is about me and what I hate,
What I like and I hope you know now about me!

Thale Clark (8)
Heronsgate School, Walnut Tree

I Am

I am my arty mother, Nusrat.
I am my dad, with extraordinary baking.
I am my brothers, Miqdad and Ali.
I am my aunty, out making wonderful food.
I am my uncle, with complicated accounting.
I am Miss Robinson, with fun maths.
I am Mrs Dimmock, learning enthusiastic English.
I am my other uncle, learning about cars.
I am Muhammed-Haamdi Somji
And this year I made 500 cupcakes for the NHS.
I am who I am because of all these people.

Muhammed-Haadi Somji (11)
Heronsgate School, Walnut Tree

I Am...

I am my mother, Joanna, who brought me into this world.
I am my sister, Zuzanna, who is always there for me and helped me through tough times.

I am the kind people in Cuba who helped me find my parents when I was lost and scared.
I am my best friend, Klaudia, who taught me how to swim.

I am my father, Marcin, who kept me safe during Covid.
I am Alicja Jaszczyk and I plan to live a long, joyful life!
I am who I am because of everyone.

Alicja Jaszczyk (10)
Heronsgate School, Walnut Tree

I Am Stacy Kanu

I am my mother, Agnes,
I am my father who moved countries just for my education,
I am my sisters who encouraged me through failure,
I am my family who worked day to night just so I can have a well-secured life,
I am my friend who misjudged me
But now supports me with a helping hand,
I am my coach who trained me for netball but never lost hope or faith,
I am Covid which took a turning point in my life,
I am who I am because of everyone.

Stacy Kanu (11)
Heronsgate School, Walnut Tree

A Recipe About Me

You will need:
100 kilograms of this numbered world.
Zero grams of a book-filled bedroom.
Ten kilograms of these soothing sounds.
Ten kilograms of these shocking potions.
Zero grams of vocabulary.
Ten grams of these 3D screens.

1. Mix it all up ten times.
A hint of these mind-blowing potions, world of numbers and this soothing sound and this shocking world.
2. Put it in the oven till you hear it click and you're done.

Kimani Njogu (8)
Heronsgate School, Walnut Tree

Me Recipe

Ingredients -
To create me you will need:
An art-filled bedroom.
Ten millilitres of kindness.
Lego.
A pinch of peas.
A hot slap of pizza.
A pinch of dark.
One millilitre of pasta.

Now you need to:
Add the Lego.
Next, add the hot slap of pizza.
Next, add the art-filled bedroom.
Mix it all up.
Then add one millilitre of pasta.
Then add the pinch of dark.
Add the millilitre of kindness.

Theadora Hyne (7)
Heronsgate School, Walnut Tree

So Annoying

Every time someone tries to help me it gets annoying.
Every time someone stops me from learning it gets annoying.
Every time someone stops me from living my life it gets annoying.
Most things in my life are so annoying.
Every time someone embarrasses me it gets annoying.
Every time someone kills me in Fortnite it gets annoying.
Every time someone ruins my hardcore world in Minecraft it gets very annoying.
This is all just so annoying.

Woody Ford (8)
Heronsgate School, Walnut Tree

People I Know

I am my caring mum, Sheena, for helping with my homework.
I am my fun dad, Peter, for teaching me how to play sports.
I am my generous neighbours for looking after me when I was lonely.
I am my enthusiastic teachers for helping me with my learning.
I am my amazing friends for being there in tough times.
I am my safe climbing instructor for keeping me safe when climbing.
I am Morgan Roberts-Fennemore.
I am who I am because of everyone.

Morgan Roberts-Fennemore (11)
Heronsgate School, Walnut Tree

I Am...

I am an indestructible brick wall when in defence
I am pet addicted
I am a needle in a haystack, always standing out
I am a controller with no brain
I am a hot-air balloon rising to the top
I am the 'X' marks the spot, waiting to be found
I am a black and white picture with colours
I am a whiteboard, sharing ideas
I am as buzzed as a bee
My hair is hazel
My eyes are as brown as bronze.

This is me.

Zachary Smith (11)
Heronsgate School, Walnut Tree

I Am...

I am my mum for teaching me to keep my room tidy.
I am my dad for teaching me to run fast.
I am my cousin for teaching me how to do a backbend.
I am my brother for always helping me out.
I am my grandma for teaching me to cook.
I am my grandad for always playing games with me.
I am my friends for always being there for me.
I am Rubi Green
And this year was the year I learnt new things.
I am who I am because of everyone.

Rubi Green (10)
Heronsgate School, Walnut Tree

Zakary Peach

I am my caring mum, Theresa.
I am my thoughtful dad, Shaun.
I am my friend, who helps me when I'm struggling.
I am my grandad, who helps me when I need it most.
I am my football manager, that trains us for football games.
I am my nan, who is always there for me.
I am my neighbour, who always is there for me.
I am my grandad, who always asks how I'm getting on.
I am Zakary Peach, and I am who I am because of everyone.

Zakary Peach (11)
Heronsgate School, Walnut Tree

I Am...

I am my grandma, who spoiled me with chocolates and taught me dominoes.
I am my grandpa, who taught me chess.
I am my dad, who taught me how to cook.
I am my sensei, for giving me my blue belt.
I am my brother, who always cheers me up when I am down.
I am my twin sisters, who passed away at birth.
I am my teacher, who helped me with my spellings.
I am me, Kristo, and I try my hardest because of Everyone giving me courage.

Kristo Kocka (10)
Heronsgate School, Walnut Tree

Who Am I?

I am my mother who inspired me when I was younger.
I am the nurses that X-rayed my nose when my mum thought it was broken.
I am my sister's doctors who got her through bronchitis and that entertained her through the process.
I am the police and fireman that came to help me when I was in a car crash.
I am the people that stopped to help.
I am my auntie, nan and grandad who I never want to lose.
I am me because of everyone.

Alexis-Mai Smith (11)
Heronsgate School, Walnut Tree

I Am Ethan Duncan-Batt

I am the hospital I was born in.
I am my mum and my dad who look after me.
I am my annoying brother who tells me what to do.
I am the boy who tripped me up and made my head bleed.
I am what made my eye unable to open and the doctor who fixed it.
I am my friends who make me happy when I'm sad.
I am my shiny Zekrom in Pokémon GO.
I am the teachers that help me learn.
I am who I am because of everyone.

Ethan Duncan-Batt (10)
Heronsgate School, Walnut Tree

This Is Me!

I am my lovely mum who helped me through hard times.
I am my silly dad who makes me happy.
I am my aunties and uncles who make me laugh.
I am my best friends Melissa and Klaudia for caring.
I am my wonderful grandparents who always look after me.
I am my kind neighbour that usually says good morning.
I am my respectful cousins to have afternoon tea with.
I am Holly Gregory.
I am who I am because of everyone.

Holly Gregory (11)
Heronsgate School, Walnut Tree

Paradise

R obber of banks, sneaker of police
U nicorns and fairies, horses and devils
B unnies and calves, puppies and kittens are the power of love
Y o bro, what's up, I'm just hanging around, well, you are hanging around in my territory.

M cDonald's is the best but can be bad
C louds so fluffy you could scream
C otton like clouds so good you wanna sleep in them.

Ruby Mccloud (9)
Heronsgate School, Walnut Tree

I Am Who I Am Because Of Everyone

I am my grandfather Zdisek who raised me on a farm.
I am my grandfather Zdisek who taught me how to drive a tractor.
I am the boy who moved to England at the age of four.
I am my coach who helped me to achieve orange belt and black belt kicks and punches.
I am my mom Anna who got me an airsoft pistol and a butterfly knife at the age of nine.
I am my dad Gregosz who got me a snake.
I am who I am because of everyone.

Adam Witkowski (10)
Heronsgate School, Walnut Tree

The Giver Of Light

I am clumsy
I am not disrespectful
I am cheery
I am not wealthy
I am myself
I am who I am
I'm Luca.

I am Mike Wazowski
I drive a motor
I am good at drawing.

I am the best footballer
I am the best at Halo Infinite.

I know how earthquakes and volcanos happen and how leaves turn green.

I love video games.

I'm Luca, the giver of light.

Luca Eggleston (10)
Heronsgate School, Walnut Tree

What I Like And Don't

I like Minecraft because I can build a zoo.
I like Pokémon because some Pokémon go moo!
I don't like spiders because they can be really big.
I like Stig of the Dump because I like the Stone Age like Stig.
I like Pokémon GO because it's like Pokémon are real.
I like McDonald's because I have a really comfy bed.
And finally, I like sleeping because I get to sleep with my ted.

Mayson Moore-Kennett (8)
Heronsgate School, Walnut Tree

I Am Who I Am

I am my kind mum, Samantha.
I am my funny dad who helps me through my hardest times.
I am my sister who raised my confidence.
I am my loving hamster, Russell.
I am my teacher who helped me succeed.
I am my best friends, Holly and Klaudia, who taught me how to have fun.
I am my doctors who healed my broken arm.
I am my cousin, Chase, who taught me how to bake.
I am who I am because of everyone!

Melissa Morris (10)
Heronsgate School, Walnut Tree

Cianne's Recipe

To make me you'll need:
Eight red pandas
A pinch of spice
Sprinkle of hyperactivity
Kindness
Friendship
Lots of salami
Lots of love.

Method:
Add friendship to a baking tray.
Next, spread some kindness.
Mix in a bowl a pinch of spice, eight red pandas, salami and lots of love.
Then add the mixture to the tray then bake it.
After, sprinkle some hyperactivity.

Cianne-Lea Mahoney (8)
Heronsgate School, Walnut Tree

Video Games Are The Best

G ames are the best,
A game makes me go crazy,
M y uncle plays games with me,
E very poem is creative just like games,
S o that is why I like games.

My favourite games are Euro Truck Simulator 2 and Roblox,
I always play as much as I can,
So that is why I have a lot of hours playing,
I play then I go to bed dreaming of the adventures Adrian will have.

Adrian Szymkowiak (9)
Heronsgate School, Walnut Tree

I Am Who I Am

I am my caring mother, Emilia.
I am my father, Krystian, who taught me courage.
I am my teachers who say I will succeed
And my doctors who helped me through my hardest times.
I am my nan, Maria, who taught me how to bake.
I am my auntie, Asia, that helped me calm down after stressing.
I am my dog for teaching me how to be kind.
I am Klaudia Gajewska.
I am who I am because of everyone!

Klaudia Gajewska (11)
Heronsgate School, Walnut Tree

All About Me

I am a book lover
I have a little brother
I am a violin wizard
I hate lizards
I am an orchestra player.

Sometimes I feel like a box because everything feels all squashed
I like majestic foxes
I like it when it's hot
And I love hot choc.

I love my family and my cat the most
My passion is science, history and to write
Although I like flying a kite.

Evie Wakeman (9)
Heronsgate School, Walnut Tree

Roller Hockey

R oller hockey is my favourite.
O ur training is amazing.
L aigie scores again.
L earn new things.
E xciting 4v4 roller hockey scrimmage.
R amming into a player.

H aving fun.
O ver skating.
C lever play.
K ey tricks to help you.
E vening training.
Y es, you can do it if you work hard.

Mason Willimott (8)
Heronsgate School, Walnut Tree

I Am...

I am my mum who helps me draw
I am my nan who makes my delicious lunch
I am my grandad who helped me when my mum was in lockdown
I am my teacher who helped me learn new things
I am my friend Cara who showed true friendship
I am my aunty who showed me gaming
I am my music teacher who showed me how to play the keyboard
I am Beau Craig
I am who I am because of everyone.

Beau Craig (10)
Heronsgate School, Walnut Tree

Happiness

H appiness is the best feeling
A nger is bad
P eople smile if you smile at them
P eople don't smile if you frown
I like to spend time with my family
N intendo Switch is a good console
E cstasy is a synonym for happiness
S uperheroes make me happy
S pider-Man is my favourite superhero.

This is me.

Murad Elfadaly (9)
Heronsgate School, Walnut Tree

Me And Thomas

Thomas is a special, fluffy, blue bear of brilliance.
Being lazy is crazy and crafts are daft.
I want to be a biologist or police officer,
Especially when it comes to running fast.
School is cool, at least I will be clever.
My bedroom's full of teddies and dogs not in bogs.
I'm a funny person with a lot of personality and ideas.
I like bikes but not hikes.

Lauren Maynard (9)
Heronsgate School, Walnut Tree

Brave And Bold

I am ridiculous.
I am funny.
I am caring.

I care what people think.
I care what I look like.
I make divine meals fit for a king.

I can swim 100 miles per hour like a dolphin.
I can climb faster than ever.
I don't know why grass is green.
I don't know why the moon comes closer every year.

I'm Leo, my name means lion.

Leo King (10)
Heronsgate School, Walnut Tree

I Am Who I Am

I am my mum Sotia who cares about my education.
I am my dad Ciriaco who can fight like a famous warrior.
I am my grandparents Chionoula, Spyros, Elena, John and my step-grandma Gabriella.
I am my whole family who all have my back.
I am my friends who are there when I really need them.
I am Alex Bosco, famous warrior protector.
I am who I am because of everyone.

Alex Bosco (10)
Heronsgate School, Walnut Tree

This Is What I Am

E nergetic
L oving
L aughter
A mazing.

G ymnast
R ainbow girl
A rtistic
C lever, cheeky, chef
E ncouraging.

M agnificent
O pera singer
W ild girl
B rave
R ider
A mazing at crafts
Y oung but eight years old.

Ella Mowbray (8)
Heronsgate School, Walnut Tree

I Am...

I am a tide, a child of the sea,
I am a boar, driven and sociable,
I am a butterfly, spreading my wings,
I am an arrow, sleek and swift,
I am a cricket, excited and free,
I am the sunrise, colourful and bright,
I am a fox, a forager and alert at night,
I am a cat, elegant but clumsy,
My eyes are lead,
My words are gold,
This is me.

Neferah Jaunbocus (10)
Heronsgate School, Walnut Tree

Smart Kid

I am a chocolate lover
I'm a car lover
I'm kind
And have a farm
I look after my birds
I look after my peacocks as well
I work with my dad
I'm a book reader
I'm a gamer
I'm a Lego lover
I'm a sweet lover
I'm a Minecraft player
I'm a chocolate eater
And a sun lover
I like summer.

Armaan Malik (8)
Heronsgate School, Walnut Tree

This Is Me

T iny on the outside but huge on the inside.
H andful of love is me.
I ntelligent I am, talented also.
S uper creative I am.

I love gymnastics and singing.
S cience is my favourite of all.

M arvellous and magnificent I am and I know.
E ach of you should call me brave and so unique.

Adrianna Tryzna (7)
Heronsgate School, Walnut Tree

Who Am I?

I am my dad who made me learn to ride a bike.
I am my mum who brought me into this world.
I am my mum and my dad who nearly died.
I am my dog that passed away in 2020.
I am my cat that has scratched me a million times on my hand.
I am my sister that fights me but supports me no matter what.
I am Max Coburn.
I am who I am because of everyone.

Max S C Coburn (11)
Heronsgate School, Walnut Tree

Me

I am my cat, lazy and aloof
I am mum, crazy and funny
I am my dad, strong and smart
This makes me... me!

I know a lot of dinosaurs
I am the tallest of my friends
I am the best at Nerf gunning.

I tussled with a Reaper Leviathan
I met a dinosaur
I time travelled.

I am who I am, I am me
I am Isaac.

Isaac Jones (10)
Heronsgate School, Walnut Tree

This Is Me

H onest and brave
O bsessed with monkeys
L oving girl
L ovely and caring
Y outhful.

D ancing
U nicorn lover
N ovember is my favourite month
G rammar is my favourite subject
A ctivities are my favourite thing to do
R abbits are my favourite animal.

Holly Dungar-Bullock (8)
Heronsgate School, Walnut Tree

Guess My Favourite Colour

The first letter is 'o', next letter 'r'
And it has the word 'range' in it
And sounds like a fruit and is a fruit.
You will find me in the market.
All people may like me,
Only one person loves me or maybe more.
Also, most things are this colour.
What is my favourite colour?

Answer: Orange.

Grace (7)
Heronsgate School, Walnut Tree

I Am...

I am my mum, she helps me in Toe by Toe and Power of Two and in homework.
I am my dad, he taught me to look after hamsters and my gerbils.
I am my stepdad, for my love of gaming.
I am my brother, Emmett, for my love of playing with young kids.
I am my grandad, for getting me hiking boots for scouts.

I am who I am because of everyone!

Tyler Howell (10)
Heronsgate School, Walnut Tree

I Am...

I am as steady as a cat on my feet,
I am on my continuous netball shooting streak,
I am a useless iron wall without my team,
I am just like a gun bullet as I shoot,
I am like a dart as I pivot,
I am a loop on a hoop as I catch,
My chestnut-brown hair flows as I pass,
My emerald eyes look out for my teammates,
This is me.

Jasmine Saidi (11)
Heronsgate School, Walnut Tree

I Am My...

I am my teacher because he made me independent.
I am my friends because they are caring.
I am my sister because she made my drawing better.
I am my dad because he made my maths and English better.
I am my mum because she gives me McDonald's.
I am my teddy because he gives me lots of cuddles.
I am who I am because of everyone!

Amelia Omonayajo (7)
Heronsgate School, Walnut Tree

An Acrostic

T rampoline lover.
H appy, hyper girl.
E nergetic athlete.
R ainbow lover.
E ncouraging girl.
S mart girl.
A mazing artist.

W indy girl.
I maginative girl.
L earning girl.
S hy girl.
O pera singer.
N aughty girl.

Theresa Wilson (7)
Heronsgate School, Walnut Tree

I Am...

I am my mum, Helen

I am my stepdad, Gavin

I am my brothers, Callum and Ewan, who (sometimes) support me

I am my grandma and grandad who taught me to ride my bike

I am my friends, Noah and Alec

I am my teacher, Mrs Timmins for supporting me and helping me learn

I am my class

I am me and I am who I am because of everyone.

Lewis Chaproniere McLean (11)
Heronsgate School, Walnut Tree

Acrostic Poem

L illy is who I am...
I nnocent
L oving
L ucky
Y oung.

B rave
E legant
R esponsible
N egative sometimes
A mazing
T errific
O bedient
W ise
I ntelligent
C lever
Z zz I am tired.

Lilly Bernatowicz (7)
Heronsgate School, Walnut Tree

This Is Me, Sofia Brown

T iny in size.
H ave many fun habits.
I love art and reading.
S easide is my favourite place to be.

I really love my family.
S ometimes I make cakes with them.

M y friends are lunatics and make me laugh.
E ating food all day long, gets treats all along.

Sofia Brown (9)
Heronsgate School, Walnut Tree

This Is Me In School

Good at school
Perfect at school
Perfect the way I am!

Good at hula hooping
Good at skipping ropes
A good friend.

Generous, kind
Love my dog, cat, cat, cat, kitten, puppy, rabbits
I have a lot!
I love my family and friends, best friends
Colours purple, blue, red, black, green, pink.

Leyah Fisher (9)
Heronsgate School, Walnut Tree

My Favourite Animal

I'm an animal, sometimes small but sometimes big.
I can be found mostly in homes but some of my kind can be found in the wild.
You can play with me if I'm not one from the savanna.
I do not fly, I live on land, not the sea.
I was used in World War One and Two.

What am I?

Answer: A dog.

Theo Smith (8)
Heronsgate School, Walnut Tree

What I Like

I like to have fun and play
I love sneaky creatures and sneaky animals
I don't know if you know I am scared of a ball
I love cute, big, small animals
I love to play games
I like sport
I love to go crazy
I love to be silly
As fast as a fox, strong as a bear
Yes, that is me
As kind as a cat.

Millie Beaver (9)
Heronsgate School, Walnut Tree

I Am...

I am a bee in the field, fast and free,
I am a dog, kind and gentle,
I am a great player when I'm with friends,
I am a chameleon when playing hide-and-seek,
I am a butterfly, small and speedy,
My hair, coloured like caramel,
My voice, soft and calm,
My eyes are my windows to happiness,
This is me.

Isaac True (11)
Heronsgate School, Walnut Tree

Who I Am And What I Like

I am taller than a flea
I like slapping knees
I'm a heavy sleeper
I love Fortnite
I do a bunch of flips
I'm a Spider-Man addict
I also like to meme
I'm a hot chocolate addict
I'm faster than sound
I'd really love to pound
I love chicken
I love pretty much anything!

Thomas Broad (9)
Heronsgate School, Walnut Tree

Happiness

H aving fun.
A nimals are exciting to see.
P ositive attitude.
P ineapples are my favourite fruit.
I like to play Roblox.
N intendo Switch is fun to play on.
E xcited for my birthday to come.
S eeing my brother.
S urrounded with happiness.

Firdaus Shouaib (8)
Heronsgate School, Walnut Tree

I Am...

I am a leaf, tumbling in the wind
I am a firework, standing out from the crowd
I am a voicebox, on repeat
I am a thorn, sharp and fierce
I am a paintbrush, exploring our colours
I am a book, waiting to be read
My hairs are springs waiting to be sprung
My eyes are like feathers, soft and gentle.

Thalia-Mae Simpson (11)
Heronsgate School, Walnut Tree

This Is Me!

My name is Aavan
My rainbow flick in football is awesome
My goal is to do a backflip
But I can do a frontflip kind of
I'm faster than an eagle
I'm stronger than a rhino
I'm braver than a lion
My favourite dog hates logs
While I hate frogs
I'm friendly and kind.

Aaron Gunasekara (8)
Heronsgate School, Walnut Tree

This Is Me!

I am a dog lover
I like animals
Book reader
I like soft
I am helpful
I am good at listening
I am good at saying sorry
I am good at listening to my mom and dad
Helpful to my mom
I am good at opening doors for adults and kids
I am good at helping kids in maths and English.

Bella Harris (7)
Heronsgate School, Walnut Tree

I Am...

I am a rainbow, developing colours
I am a fingerprint, different from the rest
I am a leopard, determined and fierce
I am a mountain climber, unstoppable and eager
I have hazel-like eyes, light and dark
I am an itch that can't be scratched, waiting to see what will come next
This is me.

Jada Boyd (11)
Heronsgate School, Walnut Tree

This Is Me

I am like a closed box.

A lot of feelings squashed inside.
M arvellous birds that I like to watch.

T eamwork is not my thing.
H aving a pet is what I like.
I like games.
E ating pizza is the best.
A nimals are my dream.

Thiea Smith (8)
Heronsgate School, Walnut Tree

I Am...

I am a big brother going on adventures.
I am a cyclist going faster than the speed of wind.
I am a fabulous basketball player,
My basketball skills are amazing.
I am an excellent piano player,
I even made my own songs.
I am a quick runner,
I run faster than the speed of rain.

Petros Gkerdouki (11)
Heronsgate School, Walnut Tree

I Am Wonderful

I like painting pictures
I like going to school
I like doing crafts
I'm always joyful
My teacher takes good care of me
I play with my friends a lot
I'm always happy
I love to talk
I'm as brave as a lion
I'm as fast as a cheetah
I am wonderful.

Ebony Davy (8)
Heronsgate School, Walnut Tree

This Is Me

T iny in size
H ave many habits
I love drawing and reading
S easide is the place I like to be.

I really love my family
S ometimes I play games.

M y friends make me laugh and smile
E ating food makes me smile.

Florence Stratford (8)
Heronsgate School, Walnut Tree

I Am...

I am my mum, who made me a gamer.
I am my uncle, who taught me to kick a football.
I am my dad, who got me my first goalkeeper gloves.
I am my sister, who made me an uncle.
I am myself, who got my first pair of football boots.
I am Alec and I'm a goalkeeper because of everyone.

Alec Price (11)
Heronsgate School, Walnut Tree

My Day

Playing the keyboard
One by one, the day
Had just begun.

Then we all sat
Down one by one,
We watched a film
After lunch.

We then ate a lot
Of sweets, then it
Was night so we all
Went to sleep one by
One, ready for the next day ahead.

Charlotte Goodwin (9)
Heronsgate School, Walnut Tree

This Is Me!

Maths is my heaven
Roller coasters go to my grave
I run faster than a train
My family like friends
This is a poem about myself
I like hammers and hospitals
Can you guess my future?
Life to death
My friends and family cheer me on
To be myself in this world.

Ben Evans (8)
Heronsgate School, Walnut Tree

Happiness

H ats are the coolest.
A pples are the best.
P ineapples are so nice.
P arents help me out.
I ce is cold.
N intendo Switch is the best console.
E ggs are good.
S nakes are my biggest fear.
S ocks are smelly.

Lennon Flynn (8)
Heronsgate School, Walnut Tree

What Is The Animal?

A beaked fellow.
Common in the Antarctic.
Waddle across their icy habitat.
Keeping their eggs off the ice.
Wings but cannot fly.
Black and white and a bit of yellow.
Very fast through the ocean.
What is it?

Answer: An emperor penguin.

William Galvin (7)
Heronsgate School, Walnut Tree

Things I Like And I'm Good At

I love playing tag with my sister
I love cats, going on walks and to parks
I like going on the slides and swings
I'm a big fan of Titanic, action games and movies
I'm good at running, riding and swimming
My future dream is to ski, snowboard and ice skate.

Jack Goldsmith (8)
Heronsgate School, Walnut Tree

This Is Me

T V watcher.
H ave a little sister.
I love school.
S ometimes play with my family.

I love friends and family.
S ometimes play basketball.

M y family and I love each other.
E xerciser.

Leila-Rae Llewellyn (7)
Heronsgate School, Walnut Tree

Me

To create me you need
A pinch of friendliness
One scoop of patience
Ten pounds of kindness.

Now you need to
Add one kilogram of love
Mix it with a scoop of patience
Stir it with ten pounds of kindness
Finally, a pinch of friendliness.

Arjun Prasher (8)
Heronsgate School, Walnut Tree

Me

H ome is very good.
A nd home is good because I have an iPad.
R eally bored in writing.
R eading is boring.
I love Legoland.
S pongeBob is the best.
O ranges are very delicious.
N o school forever.

Harrison White (8)
Heronsgate School, Walnut Tree

Me And My Friends

N ia is nice and kind.
I really like playing with my friend
A nna. She's a really nice friend.

A nd she likes to make me happy when I'm sad.
N ice.
N o spiders.
A nna will never make me cry.

Nia Shoko (8)
Heronsgate School, Walnut Tree

All About Me!

J enson is my friend
O n my way to school, I see my friends
N ot frightened
A mong Us is one of my favourite games
T alented
H ow amazing I am
A ble to think
N ow I can run as fast as The Flash.

Jonathan Cane (9)
Heronsgate School, Walnut Tree

This Is Me!

I am my mum who cares for me the most
I am my dad who loves to take me places
I am my friend who makes me laugh
I am my grandad who jokes around
I am my nan who texts me when I'm sad
I am Vinnie Girdlestone
I am who I am because of everyone.

Vinnie Girdlestone (11)
Heronsgate School, Walnut Tree

I Am...

I am amazing at basketball
I am amazing with the ball
I am a shooting arrow going through everyone
I am jumping really high, better than number 23
I am the king of the court.
My eyes are diamond-blue and
My heart is pumping out happiness.

James Diblasio (11)
Heronsgate School, Walnut Tree

This Is My Life

Animals are my favourite but my dog and cats are the best.
Animal lover is what I am.
As patient as an apple or lemon waiting to be picked.
Love all friends and family fun.
Brave, friendly, ecstatic, love reading and colour lover.
This is me!

Evie Hutchison (8)
Heronsgate School, Walnut Tree

This Is Me

Henry is my name and football is my game
I don't play for a team but that is my dream
I am a superstar central attacking midfielder
And I have always got a plan
I am a speedy central attacking midfielder
And that has always been my plan.

Henry Ives (9)
Heronsgate School, Walnut Tree

Me And My Friends

A n ecstatic girl who loves cats
N ia is the best
N o spiders in this poem
A friend is what I need.

N ia is nice and
I s kind
A nd we will never run away from each other *ever!*

Anna Knight (8)
Heronsgate School, Walnut Tree

What Makes Me Happy

S ecret Santa on Christmas Eve!
T elevision all day long,
E lf on the shelf, it's Christmas Day!
F unny jokes from my friends and I,
F ood like pasta, popcorn and cake!
Y o-yos swinging up and down.

Steffy Njenga (9)
Heronsgate School, Walnut Tree

Arsenal Is The Best Team

A rsenal is the best team.
R ude team is Chelsea.
S oon Chelsea will lose.
E normous team is Man City.
N oo! Chelsea is good.
A rsenal is not bad.
L eeds United isn't an enormous team.

Takuma Kozaki (8)
Heronsgate School, Walnut Tree

I Am Ollie

I am a good kid.

A nnoying sometimes
M ighty, fearless runner.

O ctopus liker
L ittle books lover
L oving child
I want to be a marine biologist
E nglish hater.

Ollie Reynolds (9)
Heronsgate School, Walnut Tree

Feelings

F lying in the sky
E ating my sweet pie,
E ar-dropping conversations,
L istening to whispers,
I mitating objects,
N ot listening to teachers,
G rating cheese,
S uper happy me.

Fatimah Mohammedali (8)
Heronsgate School, Walnut Tree

This Is Me!

I have hair as thick as metal
I like honey and bunnies, but normally cuddly bunnies
And I always have a big tummy
I have to bring my big tummy to the hot-air balloon
As I go high up in the sky
I shoot down, down, down, ouch! Bananas!

Sophia Sepehrtaj
Heronsgate School, Walnut Tree

Me

I am a two wheels lover
M y friend is Ollie.

T ired tiger, strong, sleeping
O n his bed
M ighty roar
M y name is Tommy Crouch
Y es, I'm strong, brave and not scared, no.

Tommy Crouch (8)
Heronsgate School, Walnut Tree

Day In The Life Of Spyros

My name is Spyros.
I'm as fast as a flash,
In football I smash.
Every day I race home.
Home to eat.
After that I go to sleep.
Then I hear my sister.
Splash! goes the jelly onto the telly.
This is me.

Spyros Gkouma (9)
Heronsgate School, Walnut Tree

This Is Me!

My name is Zenon and my age is seven
My favourite colour is red and I like to be in bed
I like to go home and play on my phone
I like to go to the chicken shop and flippy floppy likes to hop
I'm good at jokes all the time.

Zenon Murray (7)
Heronsgate School, Walnut Tree

Be Happy!

Being happy is good if someone is upset, make them happy
And you should be happy all the time
Have fun being happy, it is good to be happy
Lots of things make me happy
You can be happy at lots of things but just choose one.

Emma Shepherd (9)
Heronsgate School, Walnut Tree

What Emotion Am I?

I am always looking for clues
I sometimes carry a magnifying glass
I think that I'm also smart
I always talk
I need help but no one comes
I work hard
What emotion am I?

Answer: Curious.

Aoife Ramharack (9)
Heronsgate School, Walnut Tree

I Am...

I am a son to two amazing parents,
I am a crazy kickboxer,
I am a pet-loving lunatic,
I am an awesome author,
I am a training artist,
My eyes are ocean blue whirlpools,
My hair is like toffee,
This is me.

Noah Pykett (11)
Heronsgate School, Walnut Tree

The Boy In His Own Universe
A kennings poem

Fortnite player
Naruto watcher
Fast reader
Sweaty gamer
Music lover
Lego builder
Science lover
Book lover
Arty drawer
Switch gamer
FNF player
Basketball player
This is me.

Arvin Sandha (9)
Heronsgate School, Walnut Tree

This Is Me!

I am Levey
I am kind
I am fast.

I know my teacher's name
I have friends
I'm not a bully
I am truthful
I am helpful
I am confident.

I am me and nobody changes that.

Connor Perry (11)
Heronsgate School, Walnut Tree

What Emotion Am I?

My body is shaking
My brain is only thinking about one thing
I am practically jumping
I am starting to sweat
It looks like I have a sugar rush
What emotion am I?

Answer: I am excited. (upside down)

Mia Beamont (9)
Heronsgate School, Walnut Tree

Rhyme Friend

Brave as a bear, fast as a lightning bolt
Nobody else can be the same as me
A sugar rush kid, sweet and sour like a sweet
Tooth, a fantastic friend like a
Parent, and they all call me the
Rhyme Friend.

Mirella Biro Zengay (9)
Heronsgate School, Walnut Tree

Jolly Is Best!

J olly, jolly it is great
E than is my brother and we like to play
N o, you shouldn't do that
S o behave yourself
O therwise you'll be on the
N aughty step!

Jenson Berry (8)
Heronsgate School, Walnut Tree

This Is Me

S nack eater.
T oy lover.
E xcited for pizza.
F un friend.
A good friend.
N ever unkind.
I have friendship friend.
A chocolate eater.

Stefania Dzopko (8)
Heronsgate School, Walnut Tree

Angry Me

A t any time he comes out
N ever goes away
G ets me into trouble all the time
E rupts from my body and annoys me
R emember, always remember to breathe and count to ten.

Tyler Mossman (9)
Heronsgate School, Walnut Tree

Acrostic Poem

R oses are red, violets are blue, all I care about is me and you.
U nder the stars they shine so bright.
B elow the moonlight where the stars shine bright.
Y es that's me.

Ruby Creaser (8)
Heronsgate School, Walnut Tree

I Am...

I am a blocker
I am an impenetrable wall
I am a playmaker
I am a lion on and off the field
I am a king of a court
I have no fear
My eyes are mighty as an eagle
This is me.

Harun Abdalla (11)
Heronsgate School, Walnut Tree

This Is Me

J oyful all the time.
A ll the people in my family I love.
C urious all the time.
O h, did I not mention my favourite animal?
B ullies are always annoying.

Jacob-Junior Szukalski (7)
Heronsgate School, Walnut Tree

Sad Tristan's Riddle

When I get bullied I feel this emotion
When I get punched I feel a tear coming, about to drop down
I feel this almost every day
What emotion am I?

Answer: Sad.

Tristan Marshall (9)
Heronsgate School, Walnut Tree

Me

As mischievous as a monkey.
Eyes as brown as wood, this is me!
I have hair as black as midnight.
I have glowing skin as bright as the sun.
I'm as tall as a baby giraffe.

Dhruvan Ravi (8)
Heronsgate School, Walnut Tree

A Rap

This is me!
The best fast kid
Something else
A best maths student
And the best reader
A helpful student
And my best friends
And I'm a best student.

Adam Martisius (8)
Heronsgate School, Walnut Tree

Happy

My name is Fortnum and I am eight,
And I think break and lunchtime are great.
I want to be a builder so I can eat pizza.
I'm happy when I use the colours red and blue.

Fortnum Brierley (8)
Heronsgate School, Walnut Tree

This Is Me

A smart kid
L ikes making friends
A nice friend
Y ellow is the best colour to me
N ever been rude
A t school I love maths.

Alayna Afzal (7)
Heronsgate School, Walnut Tree

This Is All About Me

A kennings poem

I am...
A chocolate eater
A book reader
An animal lover
A mice hater
An art liker
A maths dreader
A school hater
And finally
A sweet lover.

Nadia Ceglarz (9)
Heronsgate School, Walnut Tree

The Greatest Fortnite Player

Play Fortnite.
Chocolate eater.
Seaside lover.
Likes skipping.
Loves horses.
Dog plays ball.
Rainbow lover.
Greatest artist.
This is me!

Jessica Foldesi (8)
Heronsgate School, Walnut Tree

Happiness!

Happiness is kind
Happiness is help
Some are sad, some are gentle
So everyone, be happy, happy, happy, happy
Don't be sad
Just be happy.

Eve Selley (8)
Heronsgate School, Walnut Tree

Myself

M usical
A happy boy when playing
R unning around
K ickboxing
U ppercuts
S illy but smart!

Markus Kuhle (8)
Heronsgate School, Walnut Tree

Me

I am a TV watcher and pizza lover.
I am a chocolate eater.
I am a footballer and a helper.
I am a book reader.
I am an early riser.

Xander Smith (7)
Heronsgate School, Walnut Tree

What Emotion Am I?

I'm mucky, dirty all the time
I never stop eating food
Any time I do my mum shouts, "Clean up!"
What emotion am I?

Oscar Masterson (9)
Heronsgate School, Walnut Tree

My Life

I am a...
Snack eater
Xbox lover
I love to eat chocolate
Pizza lover
I love having my iPad
And my mum.

George Orr (7)
Heronsgate School, Walnut Tree

Ollie

O llie loves trains
L oves everybody
L oves pizza
I love cookies
E xtremely.

Ollie Harrison (8)
Heronsgate School, Walnut Tree

A Recipe

A scoop of ice cream.
A dash of happiness.
A spoonful of fun.
A toy-filled bedroom.

This is me.

Chi Yuet Sharon Shum (7)
Heronsgate School, Walnut Tree

Me

This is me,
Full of love,
Kind and caring,
Love and sharing,
This is me.

May Chen (7)
Heronsgate School, Walnut Tree

The Fun Life Of Fadil

A haiku

I am good at maths,
Dash like a lightning - flash, flash
As strong as iron.

Fadil Said (9)
Heronsgate School, Walnut Tree

All About Me!

My mum says I am awesome and fun
My mum tells me I shine bright like the sun
Sometimes I really wonder, is it all true?
Or is it just a way to help me in all the difficult times that I have to get through?

I am not at all contrary
My dad thinks I am a magical fairy
With my magic wings spread out wide
I often feel like I can fly.

My grandparents call me their princess
Since I never fail to impress
They always remind me to straighten my crown
Whenever I am feeling down.

My teachers feel I am not in a million years a displeasure
And they enjoy calling me 'the class' treasure'
My friendships at school are hard to measure, I would even say impossible to measure
Since these are my greatest pleasures.

Unika Davina Parmar (10)
Khalsa (VA) Primary School, Southall

My Life

My name is Gunraj, I am nine years old and I am a boy.
I was born on November 30th 2012.
I have two sisters and one brother.
So in my life I have friends, family and more.
My favourite colour is red and my favourite game is Roblox
Which is a 3D game I play with my friends and relatives.
My hobbies are reading and gaming and art.
My favourite part of school is maths, art topic and PE.
My favourite author is Adam Blade and Pilkey.
For some reason my favourite number is twenty-one.
My favourite books are Captain Underpants, Beast Quest and Dog Man.
At school I feel happy and sometimes discombobulated.
I mostly play baseball, cricket and other games.
Whenever I'm sad I forget about it.
I really want a pen license, I try so hard to get one.

I hope I get it this year in Year Four.
I like to do maths even though it's still tricky.
I don't really like English.

Gunraj Talwar (9)
Khalsa (VA) Primary School, Southall

Magical Me

To create a magical me,
You will need... um, you'll see.
120 grams of truthful kindness
And can't forget a spectacular drop of wiseness.
If I add a single litre of determination
I get the feeling of winning in a race's temptation.
To create a magical me,
You will need... um, you'll see.
You'll need a pair of good trainers
Because my heart will run to help the needy.
Although sometimes super spectacular me is very sleepy,
But I am as determined as a mother willing to protect her child
To protect the endangered, helpless wild.
I carry the weight of litter on my shoulders
Of those who are not eco-friendly.
I would be terrified if I did harm to an animal
So I do it gently.
Don't worry if you're terribly lonely,
I will be your best friend, the one and only.

And that is a magical me,
You love me? Maybe.

Taranjot Kaur Thind (10)
Khalsa (VA) Primary School, Southall

The Magic Inside Me

The magic inside me
I feel so free
I draw all day
All the way
Outside, the breeze blows my hair
As I breathe the fresh air
Oh, I feel so, so happy
No, I'm never that unhappy
Whenever I meet my friends, my face lights up
Whenever I meet my cousins, I say, "Hello, s'up?"
My family is important, my brother, mom and dad
They make me feel better when I'm feeling sad
I love to think of songs, and sing them out loud
Writing stories and poems makes everyone really proud
The magic inside me
An important part of me
Oh, I feel oh so free.

Harleen Chawala (9)
Khalsa (VA) Primary School, Southall

This Is Me!

G urjot is my name
U nder the desk I hide with shame
R unning is what I want to reclaim
J upiter is my favourite planet
O nce I had a habit
T hermometers are not my gadget.

S abre is what I want
I need to change my font
N ight is my favourite time
G ates are what I climb
H orses are not slime.

C ables are tangled
H appiness is at the right angle
A irplanes are the best
N achos you can digest
A ccomplish asking no questions.

Gurjot Singh Chana (10)
Khalsa (VA) Primary School, Southall

My Primary School Life

I want to tell you about myself through this poem.
Growing up I went to reception,
This changed the whole perception.
Then entering my Year 1 class,
Excited to start phonics
Which was really hard as,
Now I am a master with electronics.
Nervous for Year 4 as I had no clue,
Then started Covid and left us in the blue.
Quickly moving into Year 5,
Which was really hard because of the pandemic,
I was struggling to cope with being academic,
Out of nowhere I was in Year 6,
Reality hit me like a bag of bricks.

Jaskeeratpal Kaur (10)
Khalsa (VA) Primary School, Southall

Just Who I Am: Rules

S is for sincere and loyal friend.
A is for a friend in need.
R is for rules and regulations, always follow.
G is for give yourself and others respect.
U is for understanding and being of noble character.
N is for never be late. I'm

S mart,
A dorable and
R eliable! Did you know, I am
G lamorous. I can be pretty
U nderstanding too. I have many
N ice moods and I am counting on you!

Sargun Khaneja (8)
Khalsa (VA) Primary School, Southall

Who Am I?

Jaskirat is my name
That means I am not Jane.
I do not carry a cane
Neither do I have a pet called Bane.

My brother's name is Prabhgun
He likes when flowers bloom.
I love my family
And they remember when I was tiny.

I want to be a footballer or scientist
Don't want to work in mist.
Footballer
It will help me stay fitter.

I like maths
It has nothing to do with mats.
I support Chelsea
And that is the end of me.

Jaskirat Dhaliwal (10)
Khalsa (VA) Primary School, Southall

Magnificent Me

Me, well I'm a bit wee,
I am smart and I have a large heart,
But I am also clever, now I'm better than ever!
My dream career is to be a singer and fossil digger.
At times I can be curious, but I have never been furious.
I like to care for my family and I always do this happily,
My family says I'm kind and I know I have a peaceful mind.
I always try and think positive, but during Coronavirus, I hope my LFT comes out negative!

Harveen Kaur Marwa (9)
Khalsa (VA) Primary School, Southall

All About Me

My name is Amarleen
I am so clean and keen
I am very chatty
But not very sassy.

I love yellow
Except for jello
I have a fellow
Who doesn't know the cello.

I love all dudes
As well as foods
I love gold
But hate to fold.

I'd love to be a dentist
But not a mad scientist
I won't let you push in
As I might lose my mind
And I'm not that kind.

Amarleen Kaur Chopra (11)
Khalsa (VA) Primary School, Southall

Anxiety

It is time to perform,
A light is shining on me. Only me.
The crowd is silent. Staring at me.
A bead of sweat rolls down my face,
And lands on my paper.
Another drop falls. It came out of my eyes.
It starts to pour.
It's flooding.
I'm shaking, wobbling.
Pause.
This is anxiety.
Slimy and evil.
He attacks you when you least expect a visit from him.
And leaves you, a laughing stock.

Snehdeep Kaur Dhaliwal (10)
Khalsa (VA) Primary School, Southall

Feelings Are Good

Feelings are good, I hope you know that
So next time you're feeling sad or just straight up mad
Remember this thought, recite it aloud.

You are you
I am me
We are we
I am strong and brave
I am kind
I am me and that is fine
You've got this now
So just stay strong
I am strong and brave
I am me
I am strong and brave
This is me.

Anika Sethi (11)
Khalsa (VA) Primary School, Southall

Who Am I?

Who am I?
I am me
I wouldn't change for you
So why change for me?

Who am I?
I am me
Happy and silly
Funny and wily
This is me, the real me.

Who am I?
I am me
I wouldn't change for you
So why change for me?

Who am I?
I am me
Kind and awesome
Friendly and a blossom
This is me, the real me.

Anishka Kaur Madan (9)
Khalsa (VA) Primary School, Southall

Me

I am me
Me is me
This is me
I am emotional during day and night
When I am sad I make myself sad
But what hurts me the most is me
But what makes me happy is the magic in me
All I need is somebody to feed me
Take care of me
The magic inside me
If I am happy or sad I have somebody with me, me!

Never forget you and me are in this world!

Harleen Kaur (9)
Khalsa (VA) Primary School, Southall

Me

I am me,
And I love tea,
My life is amazing,
You couldn't stop gazing.

This is my lovely personality,
I wish you were able to see it in reality,
My family is so precious,
I hope God will bless us.

Me personally,
Proceed in the world curiously,
My loved ones are passionate,
And all love is accurate!

Mineet Kaur Chopra (10)
Khalsa (VA) Primary School, Southall

The Best Poem

Mr Reed is the best
He doesn't look like a pest
He teaches us how to be the best
He teaches us to be the best by giving us tests
Mr Reed teaches us the best
And knows how to take care of a nest
He knows how to solve a quest
And that's how he's the best.

Ashmin Kaur Kukreja (9) & Baninder
Khalsa (VA) Primary School, Southall

I Am Me!

I am me,
I'm sure you'll agree.
I'm quite adventurous,
No, I'm not dangerous.
Although sometimes I can be daring,
I'm also caring.
I am helpful,
And also grateful.
I am not strange,
But I can cope with change.

I am me!

Simran Dhillon (10)
Khalsa (VA) Primary School, Southall

About Japleen

J umping
A dorable
P in
L apping
E njoying
E verything
N ever giving up.

Hi my name is Japleen
My twin is Papleen
And my sister is Japnoor.
I love to rhyme
Because I waste my time.

Japleen Kaur Kubar (8)
Khalsa (VA) Primary School, Southall

What Is Me?

What is me?
Who is me?
Why is me?
I am me!
I watch trees waving!
And birds chirping!
I look in the mirror,
What do I see?
I can see me!
Me, that nobody else can be,
Me, the only me,
Is who I'm meant to be!

Esher Bhogal
Khalsa (VA) Primary School, Southall

The Amazing Me!

I like the colour purple
I've never seen a turtle
I love dogs
I like to step on logs
I love English
I am slightly ticklish
I love pasta
I've gotten a lot faster
I like to read
I'm always in the lead.

Divleen Kaur Khurana (9)
Khalsa (VA) Primary School, Southall

The Sunflower

S mells beautiful
U ndarkened
N ice-looking
F ascinating flower
L ovely
O utstanding
W onderful
E ngaging and
R emarkable.

Mahek Khosla (9)
Khalsa (VA) Primary School, Southall

This Is Me

My name is Mehar
I love to eat pear
My favourite subject is art
I always take part.

My favourite thing is singing
As well as art
And if you want
I'll give you a start!

Mehar Moore (8)
Khalsa (VA) Primary School, Southall

About My Life

    A mazing at art.
    L ovely at helping when people get hurt.
    E ducational at writing.
e **X** cellent at being creative.

    S hy at talking to loads of people by myself.
    A lways tired.
    N ever bored.
    D aredevil when at the funfair.
    E motional at movies.
    R ecipes to help me bake.
    S ometimes annoying.

Alex Sanders (9)
Parkhall Primary School, Antrim

The Courageous Chester

C reative brain
H elpful in every way
E xcitable about everything
S mart in maths
T ruthful all the time
E ager to work
R eliable for secrets.

M arvellous all the time
O utstanding about school
O ne of a kind
R eally fun to play with
E nergetic outside at break.

Chester Moore (9)
Parkhall Primary School, Antrim

Amazing Mollie

M usical as my melodies on the piano
O utstanding as the sun on a bright summer's day
L ucky as a four-leaf clover
L oving as my puppy Ted
I ntelligent like a calculator solving sums
E verlasting with epic, amazing kindness.

Mollie Craig (9)
Parkhall Primary School, Antrim

The Amazing Caitlin

C aring, kind and joyful.
A rtistic and creative.
I ntelligent, kind and loves outdoors.
T alented in every way.
L oving, sweet and helpful.
I nteresting person and amazing.
N othing else to explain, this is me.

Caitlin Taylor (10)
Parkhall Primary School, Antrim

Fantastic Lewis N

L ucky as a soft, cuddly dog
E xcellent as the taste of a chocolate bar
W ise as an owl that hid inside a tree
I ntelligent as a bird that never stays on the ground
S mart as a cookie eaten in bites.

N ice.

Lewis Nicholl (10)
Parkhall Primary School, Antrim

All About Louella

L oving for everything
O utstanding in school
U nderstanding of other people
E xcellent at art
L ife is fun with friends
L ouella is good at gaming
A wesome friend for all!

Louella McAleese (10)
Parkhall Primary School, Antrim

Logan's Acrostic Poem

L ogan likes school
O utstanding in every way
G rateful for my family and friends
A lways happy and smiling
N ever angry in every way!

Logan Wright (10)
Parkhall Primary School, Antrim

The Crazy Chloe Acrostic Poem

C razy all day, every day
H appy with a smile all the time
L ovely to people
O utstanding in hip hop
E xcellent at school work.

Chloe Hurley (10)
Parkhall Primary School, Antrim

Felicity

        F ootballer
danc **E** r
 inte **L** ligent
        I nteresting
        C reative
        I nformation
        T alented
        Y oung.

Felicity Tarr (10)
Parkhall Primary School, Antrim

All About Me

L exie is fun all the time.
E ducational is me.
e **X** cellent at maths,
I ntelligent girl.
E nergetic Lexie likes to run.

Lexie Sloan (9)
Parkhall Primary School, Antrim

Artistic Acrostic Amiee

A wesome at reading long books
M arvellous at maths
I love my family
E ducated about things
E xcellent at art.

Amiee McDonnell (10)
Parkhall Primary School, Antrim

YoungWriters® Est. 1991

YOUNG WRITERS INFORMATION

We hope you have enjoyed reading this book – and that you will continue to in the coming years.

If you're the parent or family member of an enthusiastic poet or story writer, do visit our website www.youngwriters.co.uk/subscribe and sign up to receive news, competitions, writing challenges and tips, activities and much, much more! There's lots to keep budding writers motivated!

If you would like to order further copies of this book, or any of our other titles, then please give us a call or order via your online account.

Young Writers
Remus House
Coltsfoot Drive
Peterborough
PE2 9BF
(01733) 890066
info@youngwriters.co.uk

Join in the conversation!
Tips, news, giveaways and much more!

YoungWritersUK   YoungWritersCW   youngwriterscw